THE PERFECT GIFT

CELEBRATING THE LIFE OF
DR. HESTER RUMBERG

Copyright © 2014 by Alan & Susan Roadburg

ISBN 978-0-9811740-4-4

HESTER RUMBERG

Foreword

As soon as word got out that our dear Hester had passed away, we started getting emails, letters and cards from all over the world. These messages described Hester as unique, brilliant, thoughtful, caring, funny, a one of kind person who could not be replaced. We heard stories about her exemplifying these qualities and these stories were heartwarming but at the same time heart breaking because no new stories would unfold. And there was another common thread in these beautiful messages - that Hester always gave the perfect gift. These gifts were described as so meaningful, so thoughtful and sometimes, so funny!

We knew exactly what people were writing about because our home was filled with these perfect gifts! When Hester was following a healthy diet related to her blood type and learned that she couldn't eat chicken, on her next visit to Toronto, she came with a plastic chicken to set up in the kitchen to remind her not to eat it. When one of our kids was going on a far away back packing adventure, Hes brought a very special back pack that would help to avoid possible pickpockets. She knew that my favourite TV show was Law and Order, and on one of her visits, brought me a hardcover book that chronicled all of the different versions of that show and it included biographies of the producers and actors. When Alan mentioned not being able to make the perfect poached egg, on her next visit she came laden with the "perfect poached egg pan". And when she was here prior to our planned Alaska Cruise, she brought me this hat that had no top, but only a brim that curls around

THE PERFECT GIFT

so that it doesn't take up much space in the suitcase. She said to me "I know that you don't like wearing hats but when you're walking on the deck of the ship, and it's very sunny out, wear this and it will protect your skin, and think of me". We had a great laugh but sadly, I never got to wear that hat as Hes died in her sleep that night. These are just a few samples of "the perfect gifts".

But more importantly than these things that Hes brought, it was Hester who was the Perfect Gift in all of our lives. With all of the challenges she had, she always displayed such an incredible sense of caring for others, and through it all, she found room for laughter. She was The Perfect Gift and her absence from our lives is brutal.

This book was Alan's idea and I am so grateful to him for thinking about it and pursuing it. For those of you who were at the "Celebrating Hester" event in Seattle on October 15, 2011, you would have heard Alan present the idea and request permission to include the words of so many of you who spoke. Because many of the speeches were off the cuff, there were no written words to use, so Alan attempted to transcribe the speeches from the video. This proved to be a daunting task.

We must add a special thank you to Sarah Bleiwas, a friend of our daughter Alison. Sarah had spent time with Hes during her many visits to Toronto and to our surprise and delight she offered to complete the transcription. It was a huge job and we are forever grateful that she took it on and completed it.

Alan has also been encouraging me to get this done as it was promised so long ago. I just wasn't able to write this forward until now as it was too painful. I still have not read many of the words that people sent in for inclusion in the book as they are so beautiful but so heartbreaking at the same time. Over time I will read this book in its entirety and we are so grateful to all of you who took the time to write about Hester. Thank you!!!!

Susan

PS. As you read the stories and the outpouring of love for Hes, notice how many times the word 'gift' appears from her friends and family (I counted 20 times). How could we have named the book anything but The Perfect Gift.

The letters "CH" following a person's name indicates that their contribution was transcribed from the video of Celebrating Hester held in Seattle. So keep in mind that in many cases the contribution was transcribed from a spontaneous presentation.

To make this book available through online book sellers, we had to make it available for sale. All proceeds from the sale of the book will be donated to the Crohn's and Colitis Foundation.

Alan

THE PERFECT GIFT

Allen, Holly..8
Bricker, Marilyn...12
Burgess, Jeff..13
Cook, Laurie and Rick..17
Crosetto, Maralyn..18
Fenton, Suzanne..20
Finn, Susan..21
Fitzgerald, Waverly..22
Gandara, Bea...26
Gill, Sylvia...29
Gladstone, Arlene..30
Gladstone, Norman..35
Goodman, James...42
Hasse, Carol..43
Holmberg, Tim..45
Kimmerer, Judy...49
Klein, Lynette..54
Lieberman, Sheila..55
Matthews, Eric..56
Metzger, Jacqui...57
O'Hehir, Trisha..58
Roadburg, Alan...60
Roadburg, Alison..62
Roadburg, Susan...64
Rooney, Tricia and Budd...65
Satterwhite, Marilla...66
Satterwhite, Skip...68
Satterwhite, Zanna..69
Sleavin, John...71
Sleavin, Judy...72
van der Ven, Peter & Margreet de Leeuw..................75
Wardinger, Joel...78
Wardinger, Marisa..81
Wild Girls...84

Holly Allen (CH)

I am Holly and Hester was my neighbour 30 years ago, on Merridian Street, and there are several other people who lived on Merridian street as well, who met Hester, who are lifelong friends. I fell in love with Hester in 1971, thirty years ago. In those days I had a Vespa and Hester and I would drive around and have these incredible conversations about near death experiences, life, why we were born, what life is about, philosophizing on life in general. Having these incredible conversations while we are whipping down the streets and every now and then Hes would laugh and while I was writing this I was trying to describe how to describe Hester's laughter. Her laughter was like this intake of breath and all of a sudden her laugh hurls out of her with the exhale, just like "haaaaah". Her laughter was just such a signature. Anyway, when I met Hester I just had this sense that she was this magical person for me. I felt very known by her and I felt that everything she shared with me was a special gift. It was so revealing but I just felt so honoured to be holding that information about her and I loved that. Hester taught me a lot of things too; she was a very wise woman.

I remember one day when I said "Hes why do you always wear heels?" She said "height is power." She also told me "Holly, when you get married, be sure you marry a good person. Make sure the man you marry is more in love with you than you are in love with him, that way it will last longer." She taught me how to be generous with love, she taught me how to respect myself and to set limits, she taught me how to be self-accepting, she taught me how to stand up for myself and others when people were being criticized. One example in particular that really struck me was that she was in a situation where somebody had made an anti-Semitic remark, and she was with somebody and the person didn't say anything, and she told me about it later and she said, "it is our duty to stand up and not let that pass. To say something and to be direct about it." And I loved that. And I always do that, I don't let it slide anymore, I try to stand up and say "you know what, I'm not comfortable with that. I have friends who are Jewish, or I have friends who are gay, or I have friends who are struggling with these issues" and every time I do that I feel like I have been given a little Hester gift. So, that is all. I miss her terribly and I just want to say thank you so much, all of you, for coming so far, and to be here, for Hes. I know that she is here, I kind of feel like she is behind me every time I meet somebody that she had told me about.

Holly Allen

I believe that God (or The Universe or what ever loving energy there is in this world) intentionally put Hester into my life. Sometimes it seems that the most random meetings are the ones that have had the strongest sway and have been the most important to me both spiritually and emotionally. Hester was one of those special people, a life long friend and sister of the heart.

I didn't meet Hes until an accidental meeting after living next door to her for over six months. When we met, I knew I had met my sister – from another lifetime perhaps – who knew what caused the depth of connection. What I did know was that it felt as if we had known each other for many lifetimes. We immediately launched into discussions about near death experiences, reincarnation, history of friendships and relationships, why we were single, who broke our hearts the most, and what our favorite food was. We talked and talked and talked. We used to ride my chartreuse- green Vespa through Seattle's University district on warm summer evenings and ogle over the cute boys. Sometimes we would ride downtown on a Saturday. There would be little traffic, and we felt like two silly girls floating down the semi abandoned road, having an adventure. We usually wound up going out to breakfast, or just coffee, or whatever. We were inseparable for a time. We had so much fun.

It was the start of a rich, ongoing, deep friendship that lasted over 30 years. Hester and I would come together and then lose sight of each other, but we always knew that we would be in each other's lives no matter what. It could be a year or two without being in touch, yet we had that rich ability to pick up the exact sentence where we left off.

I miss her darling and pithy humor. I miss her shining brilliance – both intuitive and intellectual. I miss her contagious laugh that <u>always</u> drew me in. I miss her affection, her dear-ness. I miss being able to pick up the phone and listen for the first 45 minutes before saying a word (and it was almost always fascinating stuff). I miss not being able to check up on her – sometimes we would be out of touch for so long that I was afraid I would lose her; I'd call the Satterwhites or the Kimmerers and begin my hunt for Hester. I felt like I would reel her back in and our friendship would again start off with the familiar and catch up with the new.

Marilyn Bricker

In thinking about Hester, as I do all the time, I am awestruck by how she lived. She was so courageous, fun loving, smart, focused and the best friend one could ever hope to have in life.

Her book, Ten Degrees of Reckoning, is only one example of how dedicated to truth and research she was, how knowledgeable and how ably she wrote. The book exemplifies how she approached life and the deep, true feelings of friendship she held and engendered.

Susan, I can only imagine how much you miss her. I miss her too and am inspired by her. Incredibly fortunate is how I feel that I knew Hester since we were teenagers. The conversations changed over the years from "teen talk" to often more serious matters, however there was always a lot of humour shared, bringing on a whole lot of laughter. Sending you big hugs and love.

Jeff Burgess (CH)

Let me be one of the first of her colleagues to get up here. I didn't realize Hester had so many nicknames. The other thing is, I didn't realize she had so many great parties. That's really upsetting; My wife and I weren't invited to all of them, so it kind of ticks me off. I know more about your family then you can ever imagine.

We were colleagues and I spent some years at the University with her. We were friends, colleagues, and collaborators at the end, before she passed. I first met her with Mary in 1973 when I came back to the University of Washington and she was so impressive as a dentist, as a radiologist, and I think you should know, and you probably do because they had slides of some of her accomplishments in the field, but she was a hell of a dentist and a great radiologist and a great instructor, students loved her, they absolutely loved her. Part of that was because she could tell such a great story. I mean I don't know how they ever learned anything because again somebody was talking about tangents and yeah, she would often be off somewhere, but she did always manage to come back, except once she didn't, when I was having coffee with her once, she didn't come back to where she started. That was in the last year so I think that it kind of caught up with her.

She was bright, intuitive, knowledgeable, and energetic; you've heard all these things and you're going to hear more. She had a gift. She had a gift that was translated into so many different areas and it's just so damn impressive what she did with her life. I'm not going to go over everything everybody else has already said, but just to say in the last year and a half, we'd been working on some lectures that we were going to produce and put on the web in dental radiology and I was meeting with her once or twice a month with all of that over the year and a half when she developed that cold back in January, and then the cough. It was so frustrating because, the other thing about her, and God bless her, but in the end it was irritating, she was stubborn, you know. So I kept telling her "go to the doctor. Get into the physician. Go to your physician" and she didn't do it so I'm mad at her about that, I wish that she had.

Another thing is her generosity. People haven't talked about that. She had some really hard times in the last year and a half. We had many conversations about the hard times that she had monetarily - she had a lot of difficulty. And yet she would give gifts to people, and buy things for people, and help people, all the time with money. I mean she would be giving money away; it was impressive. I mean here was a woman who had very little herself, and should have had more, given who she was and what she had done in her life, but she was giving money away. Her generosity was amazing.

I'll just share one story that she told to me that I think many of you may know because she told stories to everyone here, and she probably told the same stories, but hopefully this is the right story for her. She said that when she was having her surgery for Crones she was on the operating table and she died. And during that creative time she had an out of body experience. And in death, she rose above that table and she could see what the doctor was doing, what the doctor was saying, and she actually said that she went into the next room and could see that a cart was knocked over, while she was observing this. She later told the physician about the experience, he said "impossible. Of course it didn't happen," and she said "well how do I know that that cart was knocked over then?" and the physician said "you knew that that cart was knocked over?" and she said "yes, I knew." So I am hoping, I am hoping, that that's what happened a month and a half ago. That she went there. She had that same experience. I hope that she is someplace that she can provide the same kind of love and beauty to others. That's all I have to say. I loved her very much. Mary and I loved her very much.

Jeff Burgess

Hester and I were friends, colleagues, and collaborators. I first met Hester when I returned to the UW in 1973. She was married to John and Mary and I got to know them socially and I knew Hester as an excellent radiologist and instructor at the U. I thought that she was bright, intuitive, knowledgeable and energetic. She also was a great storyteller. In fact it was this gift that made her, in my opinion, a wonderful lecturer. She not only taught students, she entertained them. This talent would also be brought to bear in the later writing of her book. In the year and a half before her death she and I reconnected over a project related to my work. We met as often as possible over tea and desert at the Tea House up on 45th. I learned much about the undertones of her book and her life. In terms of finances, she was having great difficulty. While the book was selling, she struggled mightily. But even in the most difficult times for her, she still managed to help others with donations to them, with what little money she had. And during this time she was generous with her time and willingly helped me with developing some radiology lectures, even though I knew that it was not a primary interest for her. She was that kind of person. I loved her laugh the most, I think. I hope that she rests in peace and we will truly miss her.

Laurie (and Rick) Cook

I knew Hester through our college friend, John, after they were married. One long weekend they and some other Seattle college friends came down to central Oregon to ski with us. It was the first time we'd met Hester and we all had a grand time. But the thing I remember most about that visit was the day that I didn't ski and stayed down from the mountain to be with Hester. We went on a long walk and talked ALL day. It was like I'd known Hester all my life, yet we'd only just met. She was warm, funny, insightful, caring and wonderful. I remember feeling that she and I could easily have been best friends and mourned the fact that we lived too far apart and that our lives were too separate and busy for that really to have been a possibility. All the same, whenever we did see one another it was my great pleasure. We were never really close but it didn't take much to realize what a very special person she was. I wish I had had more time to get to know her better and regret that will now never be possible. The world was a better place with Hester in it.

Maralyn Crosetto (CH)

I have so many funny stories about her but I'll let others do that. I'm Maralyn Crosetto. I'm a fairly ancient friend of Hester's, having met her almost 30 years ago, but I felt I truly met her again in 2003. I have known Hester as the fiancée and then wife of my old college friend John Holmberg. As such, I always thought she was a splendid person full of wisdom, kindness and humour, as you all know. We shared so many happy times together over the years. However, in 2003 I discovered an aspect of her character that bound me to her devotedly for the rest of her life. I'm speaking of her courage. In 2003 my partner Thomas' and my life had fallen apart in a pretty drastic and dangerous way. Out of the blue, Hester contacted us to see how she could help. I hadn't had more than a letter from her in years. Despite the fact that her own life had been completely torn apart and she hadn't yet emerged publicly from her period of grief and solitude, she reached out to us. Hester disregarded her own pain and need for privacy to offer Tommy and me assistance. She wasn't a person to pat you on the back, say "everything will be alright." For the two of us she went way out on a limb to make sure that we wouldn't fall through the cracks. I was so deeply touched by her courage and selflessness, and it was my true honour to keep this precious friend close to me the rest of her life.

Fun ran rampant whenever I spent time with Hester. She was never dull. Even when her health was bad, she would frame it within an intriguing and hilarious story. And when she felt good, well, watch out. Hours were swallowed in what seemed like a second. When I began to work with her, I thought we would settle down and get serious. I was wrong. Her spirits, always high, would warm up to the boiling point as thought after thought percolated through her mind. Our common mode of communicating was to brainstorm, whether we were discussing chapter structure for the book, research details, marketing ploys or responses to fan mail. It was actually more like a brain hurricane: ideas, both subtle and profound, poured out of Hester in a flood. The long, meandering storytelling for which she was famous, twisted into a tighter curl and I had to be on my best game to keep up.

When framing letters, we started with "bad writing" just to get something on the page. Simultaneously Hester would edit, refine, reverse herself, cross out and move forward with an explosion of perfectly modulated emotion, intelligence and care. I never saw her give a stock reply to anyone. Hester's interviews with radio talk shows and her talks at various venues across the continent were also sculpted to fit the particular audience to whom she was speaking. Her delivery, whether on the page or behind a lectern, was so gripping that it could take some time to realize the content was just as fascinating. Thinking back to the many hours we spent together, puzzling over words and ideas, what I treasure most is laughing like wild things. The girl could have done stand up. I have never had so much fun at any job and I never will again.

Suzanne Fenton

A Breath of Fresh Air. A knowing wind, blowing doors and minds open. Just beautiful; inside and out. Inspiring all who ever loved her. Telling, sharing, teaching others to live life to the fullest, as long as you live, with dignity and valour.

In the rebirth of spring, introspection of fall, joy of summer and deepest winter chill, she is in the air we breathe. Navigating the waves and currents of change with compass set to love. Come what may.

Indomitable spirit; refreshing and real, carried on wings. Over land and sea, uniting souls across the universe. Emitting rays of warmth and light, divine and golden, sunshine on shoulders.

Smiling, glowing, bursting, knowing. Wherever she is requested to be, she is. Always present when needed. In the rustling leaves on trees, the wind caressing a cheek, the sea scent wafting in and out of the moment, filling senses to capacity; a breath of fresh air. She's there, taking a stand and doing the right thing.

Until… her very last breath was drawn, stealing mine away completely. Cannot believe, cannot breathe. Lost at sea, alone. Exhaling deeply. Sighing repeatedly, the unfathomable news. But death is not her legacy. Hers is one of unwavering commitment and unflappable determination; one of hope and faith and daring pursuits. For Hester, the brave and beautiful, with love.

THE PERFECT GIFT

Susan Finn (CH)

In 1979 I moved in next door to Hester. We have been talking about her ability to find the perfect gift. This is my daughter Abby Littmann. When our kids were little she sent this book called "Hester In the Wild" so I'd like to read some excerpts from it if I could. Hester was always very concerned about us living on the East coast because of the hurricanes, and the inscription at the beginning of the book is about that.

"Hester's canoe had a hole in it. It wasn't a very big hole but the more Hester paddled the more trouble the hole made, so Hester decided to patch it. She measured, and she cut, and she sewed until her canoe was as good as new. But now Hester's tent had a hole in it. At first Hester liked the new hole in her tent, it gave her a nice view of the stars, but one night it rained and it rained some more and the more it rained the more trouble the hole made, and Hester had to find someplace else to sleep."

I am going to skip through all the misadventures that happened in between.

"For a long time Hester just sat there and watched the river, and as she watched she began to sway, and as she swayed she began to hum. Hester hummed as she patched her canoe, and she hummed as she picked up her things and stashed them onto the sea. Still humming, Hester paddled off into the sunset."

You know they say that people who hum in life are basically very happy people.

Waverly Fitzgerald (CH)

I knew Hester as an author so it's really a great pleasure to meet so many of you who knew her on a more personal level. Hester contacted me looking for help when she was writing the book "Ten Degrees of Reckoning." I don't remember who referred her to me so if you are in the room please tell me, because I want to thank you. She was a dream client for me as a writing coach. There are two kinds of writers that I like to work with: writers who are natural storytellers (so you know that that was true with Hester) and writers who work hard (because sometimes a writer can compensate for not being a natural storyteller by working really hard). Hester was both. She would get the writing down on the page so that it was beautiful and easy to follow and easy to read, and then she would work hard to make each sentence work and to be sure all the research was accurate. I never really had to do a lot. I mostly served as an accountability partner, so she could check in as she worked on the chapters.

I have to say I am delighted to hear all these stories about Hester and tangents because that was my greatest fear when I started working with her. We would get together for these meetings that were supposed to be an hour and they would go on for an hour and a half or two hours. I always worry as a writing coach when a writer is talking about the story that much, because I'm afraid they are not going to be able to get it onto paper. I'm afraid they will dissipate the story by talking about it. But that was not true for Hester. She had this natural knack for knowing how to organize the material. She figured out the design for the chapters in the book.

There were a couple of chapters that were difficult for her. One was the chapter where the accident is recounted because she had to experience the horror of that moment again and again. She worked on that chapter a lot with me. The other one was the chapter about the legal issues.

I have never been in Hester's house but I heard stories about it from her and I imagine it as absolutely filled with books, and stacks of paper. She described going through the transcripts, doing the research, talking to everybody she could find who might know some part of the story. She really did all of the work to make sure that every word was accurate and true and beautiful.

The other thing that I appreciated about her as a writing coach was that she really valued her work. Too often writers are willing to give their work away as soon as someone offers them any money but Hester knew this story was valuable and important. She wanted to get the story out into the world and to have it appear in the best possible way. She had an offer early on from a Canadian publisher who was really slow in getting back to her and didn't offer her much money, or was only going to sell it in Canada. And she said, "No, I'm not going to do that. This story deserves more. It should reach a wider audience. It's an important story and I have a duty to this story, to tell it in a way that reaches as many people as possible."

That was when the idea of self-publishing came up. She got together with Alan to shape the book--so it's nice to meet you, Alan, I've heard so much about you. She made sure it was the best book she could create. She hired a wonderful copy-editor, Kathy Bradley who is here, to make sure every word was perfect. She got an illustrator to produce the maps. She made it as beautiful as possible and this is the self-published version that came out first of "Ten Degrees of Reckoning."

But then of course the magic happened, because Hester did have this magic of being able to rally people to her cause. This is the way that she told it to me: She said that when the book first came out she wrote to six of her friends--but I would guess it was more than six looking at this room--and she told them to tell six of their friends that the book was out. Within a week or two there was this incredible buzz about her book on Amazon. People were posting amazing reviews and people were recommending it to their friends.

Hester had considered having an agent and going the route of finding that major publisher early on. But she was eager to get the story out, the book was done, and she didn't want to wait for that whole process. But she had her eye on this one particular agent, Marly Rusoff, but she had never queried her as far as I know.

So of course being Hester what happens but somebody recommends her book to a guy whose father has recently died. He is sitting on an airplane next to his wife reading the book and he is very moved by it and she asks "What is that book you are reading?" because she hasn't ever seen her husband so absorbed in a book before. And he says "Oh, it's this book called Ten Degrees of Reckoning by this woman name Hester Rumberg." And, lo and behold, his wife is Marly Rusoff, the agent that was Hester's dream agent. So Marly gets back to

New York and calls Hester and says "I really want to represent you." And that is how this really lovely book from Putnam's came out because there Hester's dream agent took on the book and made sure the story got published and promoted and distributed by a major publisher.

One other thing about Hester was that she gave the best book launch I have ever been to. It was amazing. She packed the house at Third Place Books and she had this lovely party afterwards for everybody in Seattle who had in any way been involved in the book. It holds up to me the standard of what a book launch should be like. It was a great party and a great moment. I am happy to have been a part of Hester's life. Write on.

Bea Gandara (CH)

I am also a dental colleague of Hester's and I first met Hester when I came to Seattle from California in 1982 to be a graduate student of oral medicine. And at that time she had finished dental school and was helping to teach radiology, also in oral medicine. And I realized I had met a very special person, and like other people have said, the first thing I noticed was her laugh. I don't usually laugh easily and so I just want to say that that is very, very true. And she had a way of getting through to people, to make them open up to her right away, so as a result she had friends from so many backgrounds and sometimes people just from a chance encounter would became lifelong friends. I was a dental colleague of hers as well and while I want to talk about my personal relationship with her, I must note that she loved radiology and she really was an excellent diagnostician as Jeff Burgess said, and she became a board certified radiologist when we didn't really have a real radiology program. So she was actually really good at overcoming formidable odds and so for several years she and Lars Hollander who is here tonight taught radiology together and they were truly wonderful years for the University of Washington students who are here who had the fortune of being her students in that area of learning. And so, as far as students, she really did love her students and the students loved her. Her lectures and her seminars were clear and to the point and they were always filled with warmth and humour. But, you know, every encounter with Hester was filled with warmth and humour and something as cold and sort of, I shouldn't say cold but just, you know, radiology, it was funny, it was interesting, and the students loved her and she gave a lot of time to give them extra sessions to help them prepare for boards. But beyond the art and science of radiology, she really cared about ethics and professionalism and being the doctor. It was important to her that students learned that as well.

She also was a good friend to the students. They often would come to her with problems and she was there. She was there ready to listen, to make each person feel maybe a little braver, a little more decisive, a little stronger. She did that for her students as well as her friends so she was really special. It was a real loss for the UW school of dentistry when she left.

Hester and I had periods of time when we wouldn't see each other for a year or more because she was off on different adventures, but in recent years we did have the chance to reconnect. One thing that I would like to add, that was very special to me, and this was more on a personal note, is that often we would meet very early in the morning to go around Green Lake, to go for a walk, to exercise, just to talk and share our experiences of the week. We went often for a while and over a couple of years through all the seasons. So sometimes it would be really in the dark, sometimes it would be at the first glimmer of morning, sometimes, through a carpet of petals that had just fallen off the trees, sometimes it was golden leaves. And always it was very, very special. Hester enjoyed nature very much, and I think everything sparkled just a little bit more because I was doing that with Hester. We would see a heron and Hester would say "good morning heron. Thank you for making our day better." And I think the heron stood a little taller and the turtles stood a little stouter, and it was pretty special. I can go further but I think that she really brought out a lot in just strangers around Green Lake and in the animals and all the young kids that we saw.

THE PERFECT GIFT

Sylvia Gill (CH)

I have absolutely nothing prepared except that I have known Hester since I was a little girl. I grew up in Winnipeg, and actually Susan and I were good friends, and we had our Bat-Mitzvahs together. Hester was, as I told a couple of you, the older sister who was nice to me. As we all know, older sisters aren't always nice; of course it was a whole year and half but that was a big deal back then. I lost contact with Hester and we reconnected when she and John took their first sailing trip. I wish I knew her all my adult life but I didn't. I am so grateful. We live in San Francisco my husband and I, and I come here about 4 or 5 times a year to work and I had this great connection with her since we reconnected. I hope to meet more of you, I've heard many stories about many of you and what her other family was all about, which was those friends who are here and live in Seattle and what you meant to her. She would sometimes come and stay at the hotel with me or come to stay with Charles and I - we really had this bond. She also taught me a lot about what courage is. I admired her tremendously and I will miss her a lot, but I also think what she gave to all of us is something to remember, how to approach life. She was always smiling, and that's pretty amazing considering what she went through to survive.

Arlene Gladstone (CH)

Good Afternoon, and thank you Judy. You couldn't have said more beautiful words about our precious Hester. And you've given us all permission to digress-the way Hester might have done. I would have conversations with Hester and sometimes I'd say," I love you with all my heart but right now all I want is an executive summary please." Sometimes it happened and sometimes it didn't. But the good news was she never seemed upset if I cut the conversation short and said, "OK- that's it, goodbye , talk to you later."

I am Hester's first cousin and I know that I am not the only one who adopted her as a sister. I became her "frusin", her cousin and her good friend, but before I say more I want to extend thanks to you Judy, Honna Kimmerer, Marilla and Zanna Satterwhite, Holly Allen and Maralyn Crosetto for making this happen today. I know that I speak for everybody- and from the bottom of our hearts- we are blown away. She would have absolutely loved this.

I would like to take a minute and introduce our family who is here today. First, there is dear Susan, Hester's sister, there's Alan Roadburg, Susan's husband, and nieces Alison and Marisa (and baby Tamar). I also want to introduce my husband, Hamish Cameron and my brother Norman Gladstone and my sister in law Birgit Westergaard. We four are the Vancouver family. We were the group that Hester was planning to move and be with but sadly it didn't happen.

Our family history is that our mother Bessie Rumberg Gladstone was a sister to Joseph Rumberg who was Hester and Susan's dad and to their brother, the late Ross Rumberg.

THE PERFECT GIFT

There were deep bonds. Bessie, our mother and Joseph were brother and sister and had another brother and another sister but those two had a very tight bond. Luckily when Betty and Joe got married, Bessie and Betty got along very well and that always seals a relationship forever. The Rumberg family lived in Winnipeg, Manitoba, and the Gladstone family lived in Saskatoon, Saskatchewan. That is about 500 miles west of Winnipeg. It was an overnight train ride or it was 500 miles on a sometimes unpaved road but we kept in touch. At that time we didn't communicate by e-mail or Facebook or even a phone call. If you got a phone call it was met with a What happened? Who died? That was how it was but our families somehow manage to find a connection with each other and it was very strong.

Hester's dad Joe, was a very distinguished and highly respected and much loved dentist in Winnipeg. He had a place both in the dental community, the Jewish community and the larger Winnipeg community. His wife and Hester's Mom, Betty was just a delightful extroverted person. She was a cousin of the Three Stooges which is a family practise to always mention this relationship. And with that she was able to make it very clear to us all that she could be the party girl and dance on top of the tables if called upon. That meant that Hester got from her mother and her father both a fun loving joyous spirit, unabashed humour and a very studious, respectable responsible academic side from her dad. I think the qualities from her parents were a lovely blend of the two.

In 1950 in Winnipeg there was a flood that forced women and children to be evacuated from Winnipeg. Our Uncle Joe stayed in Winnipeg to do what he could to help and Betty and her two kids, Hester and Susan, came to live with us for two months. There were eight of us in the house and we only had one bathroom which was pretty normal then. We had a wonderful time. I was seven, Hester was four. That was the beginning of decades and decades and decades of our very strong and important connection. Our family trusted the Rumbergs, they listened to them for guidance and they trusted their advice that Norman could finish high school in Winnipeg. Later, Norman and Birgit named their son Yosef after Joseph our uncle. When it was time for our parents to give me the opportunity to go away to university they said Arlene should go to the University of Minnesota because that is where Joe went for dentistry.

The family lore was of those four children who were children of Jewish Russian immigrants, three worked so that Joe could go to dental school. That was a story we lived with and I must say I've never heard any resentment from that story. They figured that Joe seemed the smartest and would probably be good at dentistry. I know there are a lot of dentists in this room and maybe you have similar stories about how family members made some decisions so someone could go on to get the university education in the years when times were tough and immigrants had big aspirations for their children.

When I moved back to Vancouver in 1970, Hester became known to my son who was then 2, as Hatter. So our communication over the years, as recently as this year, would always begin with "Hi Hatter" in the e-mails and then in return she would sign them. "love Hatter." So I can say without a doubt- and as Judy said and others will attest too- that she was there for me through all the highs and the lows.

When I visited the Rumbergs in Gimli, Manitoba, when I was 14 years old and had my first kiss with some guy, I took 11-year-old Hester aside and I said I just had a kiss, but then I went on to tell her that it was not on the lips. I can just remember this 11-year-old smiling and going ohhhh. That kind of innocent feeling of, "I get it." I don't think she did. And then I remember there were times decades later- maybe five decades later -when it was the low point in my life and she was the cheerleader as she was for a lot of us and she called one day and said that she had just been to a second-hand store in Seattle, and bought these outrageous clothes and told me to drive down to Seattle. She reported that she had just made a reservation at the Olympic Four Seasons, and said we will go there for dinner wearing outfits and speaking with different accents. I drove down to Seattle. We went out for dinner. We laughed so hard we couldn't even order our food. But there she took an occasion which was a low moment and she found a way to brighten it up for two or three hours and somehow make it look better and put everything in perspective.

From my point of view as her cousin and for me she was one of the dearest persons in my life, I loved her for her clarity, for her strength, for her directness, for her loyalty, for her humour, for her warmth, for her compassion and her support. When we got to Toronto after the sad and shocking news that she had died, we were at Susan and Alan's home and the Rabbi came to visit Aunt Betty,. The Rabbi said what you can tell me about Hester because tomorrow is your funeral and although other people will be speaking about her, I would like to say a few words about her character. And it was Alan who said and others chimed in, that it was the gifts she bought us all. She came up with amazing presents that reflected all the thought that she gave to each person. She just zeroed in perfectly on the character and the personality of each person whether it was for a baby or her nieces or anyone of us. It was truly remarkable and it was seen as one of her great features. Of course we know that most of her gifts were non-tangible, and they are the gifts that we will cherish for a lifetime.

When we got home from the funeral there was a package in our house and it was addressed to me from Hester. It was mailed four days before she died and it was this bracelet. Thanks Hatter!

Norman Gladstone (Eulogy at Hester's funeral)

Thirty-four years ago I sat in this same peaceful sanctuary to say good-bye to my beloved hero, my Uncle Joe Rumberg. Fifteen months ago I stood on the Bimah in the Shaary Tzedek synagogue in Winnipeg to acknowledge with enormous sadness the life and passing of our sweet Ross Rumberg, who died much too young.

Now, barely time enough to mend our broken hearts with Ross' death, we suddenly find our Hester taken from us, our beautiful sailor who silently weighed anchor, cast off her earthly mooring lines and sailed away during the night. No orchestra on the wharf to wish her Godspeed, no streamers from the deck to flutter a solemn good-bye, no champagne across her bow to inaugurate this lonely, solo voyage.

Only we, her friends and family who loved her, cared about her, cheered for her and cherished her are left with our grief and memories in the wake of her life that has just set sail, a life lived with grace, generosity, humour, perseverance, dignity and enormous courage. For Hester to leave without a word was so completely out of character that I am standing here wondering if she fully intended to leave us guessing as to what her next chapter would be. And words were what Hester did so well, either spoken or written.

We could never accuse Hester of brevity. We could never say that she told a story without encompassing a myriad of facts, character sketches and complicated situations that seemed to defy gravity. Words. That was her forte.

She provided us with information that kept us enthralled, enlightened and with more detail than we ever thought we wanted or needed. But, she had an uncanny, mesmerizing delivery, punctuated with laughter that riveted our interest, compelled us to listen and piqued our curiosity. And when it came to the written word, what better proof do we need of her talent than to look upon her book published under the Penguin mantle. Ten Degrees of Reckoning. A harrowing tale of a family lost at sea, the survival of Judy Sleavin and the triumph of human will in the face of adversity.

In a way, it is Hester's story, but not quite. The triumph of the will to overcome a series of setbacks and disappointments by looking at life through an optimistic kaleidoscope and combining that with the courage to carry on was what our dear Hes was all about. What can we say of another as we look back upon a person's life, when we take the starting point of being four years old and seeing that person through to their mid-60's, which is the length of time I knew Hester.

The difficulty lies in the fact that a person is not static, but changes throughout a lifetime, so to try to freeze frame one particular moment and say that that is the true essence of a person is to ignore a multitude of attributes that develop and flourish in either the preceding or later years of life.

The difficulty in trying to describe Hester is that she was a contradiction in so many ways. Fragile and vulnerable on one side or a force of unrelenting strength of purpose, on the other. She always kept us guessing. But, to be certain, the contradictions being what they were, Hester never did things in half measures. If she was at the top of her game or at the bottom, it was all or nothing. This, I have found to be the common thread in a lifetime of knowing her. If Hester was your friend, she was your fiercely, loyal friend. If Hester were your teacher, she would not relent until you understood and achieved success. If Hester were your navigator, then she would take you safely to the harbour.

The great Winnipeg flood of 1950 sent Auntie Betty, Hester and Susan to Saskatoon, while Uncle Joe stayed home as part of an army of volunteers that built dikes to try to save the city. The unexpected bonus for my sister Arlene and me was that we gained the world's most entertaining aunt and two ready-made playmates for a period of two months. That was when the bonds of love and friendship were formed and remain in place to this very moment and will endure well beyond the here and now.

But, it wasn't until our teenage years that Hester and I became very close, the unfathomable prairie distance separating Winnipeg and Saskatoon shrinking with the CNR's overnight Super-Continental or the liberation one obtains with a newly acquired driver's licence. And it was during those formative years that I discovered by observing Hester that one could be enormously popular while resisting the temptation of being one of the pack. She was, without a doubt, her own person and an independent thinker, qualities I admired greatly. It was also during those years that the first diagnosis of colitis occurred with the sobering effect that teenage health could not be taken for granted and that compromises had to be made throughout one's life.

Hester's father Joe had a tremendous influence on her life, as he did on Susan's and Ross's. He inspired her to follow a career in dentistry. But, it was more than that. He imbued in her the courage to carry on, even when life was precarious. Our Uncle Joe, first a Captain and then a Major in the Canadian Dental Corps attached to the illustrious Fort Garry Horse Regiment, who survived the sinking of the troop ship Santa Elena carrying 1,900 Canadian soldiers off the coast of Algeria on November 6, 1943.

Our Uncle Joe who went from Sicily to the heel of the boot of Italy to the withering battles of Ortona and Monte Cassino, to Arnhem and the liberation of Holland. Our Uncle Joe who knew something of enemy fire and yet always managed to find a humorous anecdote in the midst of the most daunting of situations.

And Betty, Hester's mother, our Aunt Betty, who goes under the moniker of "Bubs" to her grandchildren, first cousin to the original Three Stooges, a true fact she would very much like widely known. Aunt Betty, whose spirit and thirst for life was and is infectious and inspiring, if not a little unconventional. "Tell it like it is, but tell it with passion" would be emblazoned on the imaginary t-shirt I would give you, my dear Aunty. Independent thinker, woman in her own right, graduate of Minnesota's St. Cloud Teacher's College, a woman who does not fit the mould and could care less and showed Hester – and all of us – that you must be proud of who you are. We sit with our Aunt Betty in shared grief on this day of saying farewell.

There was never a single career path for Hester. She was, over the years a dental hygienist, a dentist, a university instructor, a maxillofacial radiologist, a sailor, a navigator, an educator, a deck hand, a boating safety instructor, a researcher, a writer, a published author. A graduate of the University of Manitoba and the University of Washington, Hester was always a bright light, a woman of great intelligence and insight. The friends she gathered around her adored her and kept her safe. In particular I am thinking of the Kimmerer's and Satterwhite's who became Hester's Seattle family and who, in turn, adopted her as one of their own. It is this incredible, indestructible friendship that many of us are so keenly aware of and wish to acknowledge with heartfelt gratitude. Judy, Rob and Honna Kimmerer and Skip Satterwhite are here with us today, Marla, Roland and Zanna Satterwhite and Jada Kimmerer in spirit.

While living in Seattle, Hester's former husband John introduced her to sailing. If there was ever the proverbial duck to water, it was Hester taking to a sailboat. Not bad for a girl from the prairies whose waterborne perspective was probably shaped by a motorboat on Lake Winnipeg. While that body of water is not insubstantial, rating right up there as one of the largest fresh water lakes in the world, the idea of sailing on it during summers spent at the cottage in Gimli was a foreign a concept. It was one of those things that in theory could be done, but it was just not the type of thing prairie people did.

No, it was under the idyllic conditions of Puget Sound in the Pacific Northwest where our intrepid sailor gained her sea-legs. And not easily. In the early years most of Hester's time was spent hanging over the rail, questioning her sanity of embarking on such an endeavor. But, she persevered. It just wasn't in her to give up. And eventually, but not without setbacks, she found that she could not only keep her dinner down, but she could sail a boat with competency and confidence.

A good friend of mine once told me that few people understand what it takes to be a real sailor. Those of us who find comfort on solid ground while admiring white sails on the ocean from afar do not fully appreciate both the perils and the peace sailors face.

For those who sail out of sight of land, a boat becomes a bubble with mere centimeters of a hull separating them from the depths below. The romantic side of wind and wave is, in fact, an endurance contest between the skill of maneuvering a boat over a moving body of water and the unpredictable forces of nature. There is not a lot of room for mistakes. Wanting to call the whole thing off in the middle of a South Pacific gale and a 1000 kilometers from land is not an option for any sailor and the voyage must be seen to its end.

I really don't know what kind of courage it takes to make such voyages as Hester did to Hawaii, Vancouver Island and New Zealand, but whatever it was she had the right stuff and had our respect and admiration in achieving what she did. New Zealand held an enormous focus in Hester's life for it was here that her friend Judy Sleavin was washed ashore, having lost her family in the sinking of the Melinda Lee. It was this tragedy that irrevocably altered Hester's life.

It was because of this seminal event that Hester eventually came to write "Ten Degrees of Reckoning", a book that consumed her every waking moment for several years. It was Hester's will and determination that saw this book through to publication so that the story of a travesty of maritime justice, the warning to other sailors and the resiliency of the human spirit could be told.

How do I tell in a few passages the story of our beloved Hes? How do I tell you how she loved her mother, her sister Sue, her nieces Marisa and Alison and nephew Joel, Sheila and Steve and all the Lieberman cousins from St. Paul, Minnesota; her cousins Arlene, Hamish, Daniel and Naomi, of blessed memory, Birgit and Yosef from Vancouver? I know how much joy she felt in welcoming great nieces and nephews. How do I tell you how she reveled in the idea of being an aunt and a great aunt?

How do I, standing here today convey to you the depth of her being, the warmth of her soul, the intelligence of her mind and the generosity of her heart? What can I do, but tell you that to know her was to love her.

Oh, how she leaves a gap in our lives. Oh, how she makes us cry with her leaving. And, oh, how she will make us laugh sometime in the weeks, months and years to come as we recall her beauty, her spirit and her stories.

Sail on, dearest of cousins, sail on daughter, sister, aunt and friend.

Sail on, Hester. Sail on.

James Goodman

The first time I met Hester was at a reading in San Francisco she did for *Ten Degrees of Reckoning*. (My wonderful friend, Maralyn Crosetto, had clued me in about Hester and the book). I had a good talk with Hester then, but it wasn't until Maralyn's surprise birthday party that I had a chance to really spend time with her. Even though we only met twice, she could easily have been one of my classmates from Colorado College who I still feel a remarkable connection with after almost 40 years (Yikes!). I am both sad and angry that we are denied her company, and I truly regret that I won't get to know her better through the loving eyes of her many friends.

Carol Hasse

I will always be sorry that I was unable to attend Hester's Celebration of Life. I would have loved to have heard the tributes and stories about Hester's courageous and remarkable life. I am sorry to not have met her friends and family, to feel the comfort and strength that comes from sharing grief and love and laughter. I am mostly sorry she is no longer with us. I had imagined more conversations, more teaching and sailing together; just more time with Hester.

I first met Hester in 1984 when I made sails for her new boat. We shared a passion for sailing, for the cruising life, for wanting peace and well being for all, and an ongoing hope for the healing of heart and soul that can be experienced in nature. Our lives would intertwine periodically as teachers in women's and co-ed sailing seminars — where she inspired all of us with her stories and knowledge. I also learned of her health challenges and her indomitable courage and compassion. Hester's phenomenal intelligence always showed in her humor, her speaking, her teaching, and her writing. Her absolute brilliance showed in her gift of combining that intellect with her ever kind, clear, and caring heart. Perhaps Hester's greatest contribution to the cruising community is her work with the Sleavin Family Foundation. Her insightful, touching book about their tragic accident at sea will further safety on our oceans and continue to make positive changes in maritime regulations, communications, and awareness of vessel traffic concerns. It will bring compassion and understanding to bear regarding this heartbreaking event.

Hester's accomplishments are many, and the lives she's touched…many more. To me, Hester was an angel come to Earth. Her generous, brilliant, fun-loving soul, her compassionate, kind heart, her grace and strength, and her courageous perseverance will always inspire me. Safe sailing, Hester!

Tim Holmberg (CH)

I am Hester's nephew, and my dad was John's older brother. I first met Hester when I was in kindergarten and we came out here to Seattle when my parents did a sabbatical. We met Judy and Rob, and I have really known her since then. We intermittently had family vacations since then, and then it was in the middle of college when I truly got to know her better, living in their basement for half a year, then following that living in about 7 different apartments and houses throughout Seattle for the next 10 years she usually helped me move into, rearrange, decorate, and even spending a period on one of their cruises on the boat with them.

Thinking through what it is about Hester that I can say - There are endless thoughts that come to mind, that she shared her ability to throw a party, the party she threw for us at our engagement, reminded me of this most amazing skill of knowing every friend of mine's name, as well as how I knew them. As she threw this party and people came into the house she knew exactly who they were, would ask a specific question about that friend she may have never met. And gifts - she must have had a day of sending out a bunch of gifts. Right before she left on that trip, my little sister, who has a 6 month old baby, received this little rubber giraffe that she has been chewing on since and I just recently learned that Molly got that the day before learning that Hester passed along. So she was always thinking of special gifts.

I picked out a few specific things that really come to mind. First, I am going to say there is this little hanging fruit, and that is laughter. Everybody in my family who I asked "what would you like me to share" immediately came to mind that laugh, a sort of xylophone of laughter juice bursting out right at you, crashing over you like a wave that just had time to settle down again before the next one just came right at you. Whenever I think of Hester I'm hearing that laugh in my head, this constant sound that keeps resonating.

The next is really her sense of enthusiasm for adventure. She was an incredible adventurer and really experienced so much adventure, and ability to create magic in that adventure. We took a trip when we were living in Salt Lake City at the beginning of high school up to Idaho, and John and Hester came out from Seattle. It rained the entire time and I remember each day as we thought about maybe having a sunny day, and dreamt of that, and in the morning we would sit under a wet tarp and sip our hot liquid and she would just look up and "raaiiiiin, raaiiiiinnn, raiiiinn," and just burst out, followed by a full laugh, and it was the happiest amongst everyone in spite of this miserable situation.

I was also, as I mentioned, lucky to see her at home on the boat as I got to spend a few months while living on the boat with John and Hester, and see how she was also able to just create magic and excitement and exploration. She would just plan these forays into these unknown islands, into villages with teeming kids all through them. She would have a week planned out of how we were going to engage and create a whole narrative of the stay, and really make the magic of a lot of those adventures.

As I move to the last thing that comes to mind for me, Hester was a great storyteller, and she was a very detailed storyteller, but to me she was maybe more importantly this detailed listener, and I think both in her storytelling and her listening taught me to be a better listener. For a kid coming from the Holmberg family, where we're not much storytellers, I was not accustomed to the long and meandering tracks that she would sometimes go on. Certainly I would spend a lot of time listening to her stories, and her memory was just tangent upon tangent going off, and she taught me to learn to follow those because she, more than anyone I can remember, could always in a second cut back right into where she was, and if you weren't paying attention you could miss the entire reason she was off wandering over there. I would always just wait for her to not remember where she was going back to, and I would redirect, I would try to ask a question to try to get her back on track, and sometimes she would look at me with a gleam in her eye, a challenge almost.

More than her stories she was an amazing listener. During the time in my life when I was around her the most, the middle of college through the next ten years, wandering far from home, from family, exploring, learning about myself, calling my parents once every few months, I was regularly checking in with Hester. She and I had so many amazing conversations on growing up, on relationships, on death, on love, on all of those things that all of you shared with her. She has really taught me to be the sensitive and patient listener that I try to be when I can. So I want to end with a toast, anyone here who has a child who has ever told a story to Hester, told a joke to Hester, and had her burst out laughing. And anyone who was a child, or a kid, who told her a story and had that wave come crushing over them, or anyone who knew a child who had that, I'd just like to raise a glass to Hester and to the strength that she gave each person that she responds at a story, or joke, with this beautiful wave of laughter, and makes you stand a little taller. Thank you all for being here, it is wonderful to share this with you.

Judy Kimmerer (CH)

The reason for this get together, not one to one but together, all together, is we wanted to honour Hester's words and we wanted to make this more of a storytelling opportunity. We all know how good a storyteller Hester was. And her stories started here and they went waaaay around and they finally came back to an end. So we're going to do the same thing today. We want tangents, we want circuitous, we don't want to get to the end very fast, and we certainly don't want to leave anybody out. We all knew Hester in different ways, if you have a tiny little story or a long thing to say, we want to hear it because we all knew Hester in such different ways and she had so many parts to her life. And we don't know them all, so hopefully we're going to create Hester's story and walk away feeling that we know her a little bit better than we did before and feeling so much love for her. We are doing a video because Hester's mother Betty is turning 100 this month and she could not be here with us, so hopefully she will get this and enjoy it along with other folks who couldn't be here.

My thoughts today are going to be a collection of my relationship with Hester as a very good friend and what I would call her Seattle family. I think that would be her second family, and I believe there are others who also consider her their second family. It seems her loving and thoughtful nature gave us all permission to let her slide beyond the concept of friend fast to being a sister, a mother, a daughter, or an aunt. Hester entered our life when she became our neighbour's girlfriend. She moved in next door and within no time the floodgates opened. You can just imagine these two houses, children running through the fence, back and forth through the front yard. Our two homes became a sort of commune; I called it a little bit of heaven. Picnics and going on sailing adventures with them and of course Hester's goodies and these wonderful events where we would eat together.

The birth of our second daughter Honna, was life changing for Hester. Honna became Hester's baby too, and it was Honna who nicknamed Hester 'Ha Ha' when she first tried to say her name. I have one recollection that I just love, it was a time when Jaida and Honna were 7 and 11, and Hester helped them put together a very intimate anniversary dinner for Rob and I. She took them to the store, she helped them create this wonderful beautiful presentation of food and they learned first-hand about her hospitality skills, and we were so grateful that someone could fulfill a role like that for us because our mothers were far away from us in Rochester, New York. And this event was repeated over and over again, even on our 25th wedding anniversary, when Hester helped create a fantastic party at their house.

This story can be repeated many times over as we knew Hester to be the consummate party organizer where nothing was held back. In fact I would say Hester knew how to create fun, not just have fun, and she knew about making memories the ones we get to keep forever and the ones we get to cherish at times like this and far into the future. Hester was more than a sister for us as she was a mental health expert, a family counsellor, a medical adviser, she was always the best person to talk to if you had a problem, and her perspective was so invaluable since most of our problems were about each other. She loved and knew us all inside and out and could give meaningful and loving, and yet objective, insight. She seemed to have this bank of wisdom, probably from her own personal experiences, but also from all the other friends and family she undoubtedly performed this role for. Little do we know how much our lives are interconnected by the wisdom of Hester.

When Hester's marriage dissolved she moved even closer into our lives. My brother skip and his wife Marilla had an empty nest and a lovely apartment in their home which they offered to Hester. Their house mate for the past many years, Hester was elevated to a whole new rank in the family. Our lives could not have been more intertwined, more personal, more dependent. Hester helped us navigate every joy, every sorrow, every disaster, every moment of anticipation. She loved watching Stu and Zanna's family grow and couldn't wait to see the expected child Evie and see the darling Posy become a big sister. This love we felt was a spillover of the same joy she expressed over and over and over again as she dearly loved talking about Marisa, and Joel, and Alison, and their families, Betty and Susan and Ross, and her all-loving Vancouver family.

In the months prior to June of this year, Hester knew she was not well. Despite that, she managed to keep her spirits high. Recently our best time with her was our vacation to Cancun, Mexico in February. We enjoyed time on the beach and were surrounded by sun, family, and an immersion in our own simple paradise. She was our Spanish translator and storyteller as it brought us trips to far off places, symbols of her adventure for life, and embracing all people regardless of their differences or inadequacies.

Hester, my dear you couldn't be more in our hearts now and for always. You have shaped us, loved us, trusted us, and most of all shared the adventures of your life with us. You are now on the greatest adventure of all and I know your sails are full, hoping that you're seeing as your destination the faces of lost loved ones and the truth of the universe. Bless you as we all wave goodbye only to await seeing your face again one day as we too make the same life's journey.

Judy Kimmerer (CH)

Ok so this is the end. A lot of planning went into this. Kimmerer and Satterwhite came up a lot and there were a lot of people that helped. I have to say Holly Allen was just tremendous. In so much of this, lots of details and beautiful thoughts of what would be best for Hester and how Hester would have wanted this party to be with the best champagne et cetera. I feel like we planted a seed, we hoped we'd get some kind of bouquet out of this event; we'd get something that was wonderful. And I think we got this gorgeous, gorgeous bouquet from all of you speaking and sharing. Thank you very, very much. I want to end with something that is at the back of this program. These are Hester's words. I was putting something together and I thought, "well, she wrote a book. Maybe there is something in the book that is worth saying." And I found this passage, it is near the end of the book, and it says:

"None of us get to choose how we are going to die, or when for that matter. But each of us can take a page from Judy's page and decide how we are going to live. As trite as it sounds, it is still a day at a time, sometimes just a step at a time. Certainly some days or steps falter, some days or steps go rather jaunty, leading to a skip, a more complicated step, and on the very good days, a tango."

And can't you just see Hester doing the tango. She did it so many times in our house. Here's to Hester.

Lynette Klein

When I met Hester the first time, I learned immediately she was a person with the innate gift of focusing her whole self -- heart, mind and soul -- on the person with whom she was speaking. Oh, it was such a good feeling to be in her presence! I think we all yearn for truth, soulful energy and expansive ideas, and Hester so naturally shared that and more. She just connected – person to person - with a sense of ease and joy. My visits with Hester were limited, but I feel deeply blessed our paths crossed and very grateful to the Satterwhites for making introductions.

Sheila Lieberman

There is so much to say about Hester. Our mothers were sisters, as a result at an early age Hester, her mom, dad, and siblings Susan and Ross motored down to St. Paul Minnesota for holidays and special occasions. Our family in turn either drove or took the train to Winnipeg to celebrate Rumberg lifecycle events. Hester always had an affectionate loving relationship with her Aunt Elsie, Uncle John and Cousin Penny. In fact she was the expert on family genealogy. I could always go to her if I wanted more information on relatives, our most colourful being the Three Stooges. Hester taught us so much when struggling with her health challenges beginning as a teenager. She taught us how to face adversity with courage, determination, and perseverance beyond what seemed physically possible. She always had the gift of connecting with friends, relatives and colleagues, always wanting to know more about us rather than withdrawing into herself. And Hester was a romantic. She dreamed and fulfilled more possibilities than any of us could imagine – a dental hygienist, teacher, dentist, dental radiologist, accomplished sailor, devoted daughter, sister, sister-in-law, aunt, cousin, friend, and author. We will miss her sense of humour and wonderful gift of words and presence. We will miss how she taught us to embrace life. Rest in peace dear cousin, we will never forget you.

Eric Matthews (CH)

I want to take, in the spirit of Hester's circuitous routes, two little threads. The first thread is a very good friend of ours is sitting at home reading a book, and this book was given to him by a friend who is a teacher, and that teacher somehow, I'm not sure exactly the connection, teaches the children of John Sleavin's brother, Mike Sleavin and Tahoma, and their children. So he is reading this book. So that's one thread. Then the next thread is that there is this person, in Japan, which is me, in the coast guard, and I happen to be asked to go to Korea to look at a vessel named the Pan Grace to see if I can find anything out, perhaps interview the crew to find out what they may know about this terrible accident that happened off New Zealand. I was fortunate enough to be able to find a little bit of paint on the bow of this vessel that happened to connect the Pan Grace to the Sleavin's vessel, the Melinda Lee.

Getting back to my friend, he called me, and I had no idea that the book had been written, and he called me and said "Eric, I'm reading this book" and he shared with me about the book being published and I was then able to get in touch with Hester. We met, and we had lunch, and I got to know her, and her sweetness and her humour and her laughter, and she was just a real jewel to get to know. She came to Bainbridge Island where we live and was nice enough to do a book signing and a book reading there. It is just a small tasting of who she is, she just kept reaching out to everybody. She was just pleased to get to know anybody. And I was just pleased to be able to contribute a little bit towards the story. It was just a treat to get to know Hester and she is going to be missed a lot.

THE PERFECT GIFT

Jacqui Metzger

It was a heartfelt gathering to honor and remember Hester. She meant a lot to me even though we didn't see each other very often, each visit was quite memorable. We were both Jewish and that was a bond that added to our connection here in Seattle. I also so appreciated her energy, her caring, intelligence, humor, her laugh, her persistence, her courage and of course, her stories.

And she spoke often of you both, marveling at your generosity and support as she struggled to write her book, finish the writing and find a way to get it published. That experience too was, in a different way, at least as interesting as the story she told. She gets a (big) gold star for staying with that (unbelievable) process.

I also heard her talk at the First Place Book Store book signing here in Seattle... she was fabulous. Articulate, engaging, knowledgeable, and told her story succinctly with enough detail and humor to touch all present. I can only imagine what her loss means to you both. May you find comfort in your memories.

Trisha O'Hehir (CH)

I am Trisha O'Hehir, a friend of Hester's for many years. I was born in 1947, the same year that Hester was born. In 1967 I graduated from dental hygiene at the University of Minnesota, the same year she graduated from dental hygiene at the University of Winnipeg. I didn't meet her until 1976 when I took a position at the University of Washington and she was a dental student and a faculty member. Tim I think has left, but she practiced on me before she went off on those trips and organized things to do with people in foreign countries. I had never met her, when she came up to me, introduced herself and said she had a travel proposition for me. She had a certificate for a free weekend at Lake Chelan, but she didn't have a car to get there and I had a car, and wouldn't I be willing to share this certificate and go with her. Well, she was a perfect stranger, but she was a dental hygienist, so I thought she couldn't be all bad, so I said "okay I'll go on this trip." The one thing she didn't tell me is that we had to sit through 90 minutes of a time-share sales pitch, before we got our free weekend and free meal. But that was okay we laughed through it and they knew from the get-go that neither of us would buy a time-share so they let us out early with no purchase.

That's how I met Hester and the adventures just kept going on. She never did anything without adventure, and she loved travelling. I knew her during the time I lived in Seattle and then I've been in Arizona 30 years and we have still stayed in touch of course with email and phone calls, but we've always met in different places. I was able to invite her to be a featured speaker at several dental meetings in Phoenix, Tucson and Las Vegas. And then I would meet her around the country when she was speaking on Safety at Sea. I even spent a couple visits with her in-laws in Florida when they were her in-laws. So we had lots of different adventures, different places, but we always managed to keep in touch because of her love for adventure. It was fun to see how she included adventure in her life. Her life was never dull, never ordinary. Her sense of adventure began as a child, something I never knew, but, learned in Toronto from Hester's family at the funeral. What we in Seattle thought was just storytelling among us, she did as a child! It started long before we knew her, and she loved telling stories, and we all loved hearing those stories, so isn't it fun we can turn the tables on Hester here, and tell stories about her.

Hester loved parties. We had so many fun parties. Hester would plan them when I was in Seattle. I would come to Seattle when I lived in Port Townsend to stay overnight to catch a flight the next day to somewhere. She had one of those big parties when I was jet lagged coming back from the UK and somehow I'd have to rally for her parties, which wasn't always easy. All I wanted to do was sleep. Rob where are you I think I saw you in a kilt one time. It was just a plaid blanket, but it was a tribute to my return from Scotland that time.

Isn't this a perfect setting, I have to ditto Arlene with thanks to the Satterwhite's and the Kimmerer's for this wonderful tribute to Hester in a place that she loved. She would love this party, wouldn't she? Hester will always be in our hearts and I will treasure all the wonderful memories of adventures I was lucky enough to have with her. Thank you all, it's been fun.

Alan Roadburg (CH)

I don't actually have a story to tell but I have a little message to deliver. We have been giving a lot of thought to Hester talking about her many qualities, and what we love so much about Hester. One of the many things that we thought about was that she was magnificent at giving gifts. She would always seem to give the perfect gift. In view of all of this as well, on the website a lot of you have written some incredibly beautiful things in memory of Hester. We've received some amazing and heart-wrenching emails on your relationships with Hester.

So we are planning to produce a book. Our plan is to take all of the emails that we received, and all of the comments you people have made about Hester, and compile them into a book. It will be called "The Perfect Gift." It is a double meaning as we all know. On the one hand Hester herself for us was the perfect gift, and on the other hand Hester personified the perfect gift. She would come to visit us in Toronto and she would say "Alan I bought you this knife for slicing tomatoes." Well I'm not a great cook but a knife for slicing tomatoes! I have tell you that was the perfect knife for slicing tomatoes. She had the capacity for delivering the perfect gift. So here is our request. I would like you to please write something, your stories from today, whatever it is you want to say about Hester. We will use your and comments to create The Perfect Gift.

Finally, once again, I can't say it enough, thank you everybody who put on this wonderful session. It is funny, but I have to say from my heart, I was a little worried about today. We went through grieving, and it was a cloud over Susan's head for a long time. The one saving grace in our family was having the grandchildren around. This helped to pick Susan up. I was worried that now as we are starting to have this cloud slowly start to lift, we will have to go through it all again. But I have to say that we haven't really gone through it all again. I want to say thank you all for putting it on because I think it was a very uplifting and a very positive thing to do in the memory of Hester who we all love. Thank you.

Alison Roadburg

Dear Auntie Hester,

It's hard to imagine where you are right now. I have attempted to write this letter on many occasions, but either the words wouldn't come, or my emotions got the best of me. On my walk to school this morning, the sun was beaming, illuminating a city that that sees so much grey. The feeling of excitement, hope and satisfaction ran through my body. I knew that this was the day that I could write to you.

I have been trying to figure out why it has been such a challenge to write this letter. I think often how much I wish I could just pick up the phone and call you to chat, and yet writing to you has proven nothing but difficult. I am feeling blocked because it is nearly impossible to translate my personal pain and loss into accurate words. The English language is just not that sophisticated.

I just re-read all of our email correspondences over the past few years. Most recent was the planning of my visit 2 summers ago. It feels like yesterday. Though you were really sick, probably more than any of us knew; you put your life on hold to accommodate me. You took me to goodwill, to a restaurant that employed at-risk youth, on a beautiful walk around the lake, and bought the entire gluten free stock at whole foods! You nailed it. You are such an incredible and inspiring human being, and I just wish I told you that more. Your hugs and kisses had passion, strength. As a frequent receiver, the love was felt - it was real.

Now that I am an aunt, to five absolutely remarkable kids, I can only aspire to be half the role model you were to me, Marisa and Joel. The presence you assumed in my life is really hard to describe. You were the cool aunt, the person who would whole-heartedly listen, who understood, and who gave. You understood me in a way that others didn't. You just got me. You encouraged me to go after my dream, and auntie Hester, I'm living it! I know you would be so proud of me. I'm working towards my Masters in a subject that is beyond fascinating to me. When I got my first acceptance letter, I was trembling. I was on the phone with my mom, and I remember saying to her, 'I wish I could call auntie Hester to tell her.' I think that a lot.

I believe that you are in a peaceful place. I believe that you are happy. And I believe that we will meet again. I cherish you, I love you and I miss you more than words.

Susan Roadburg (CH)

I did not prepare anything to say as I didn't think I would have it in me to do so. But I must say a few words. How can I not? Firstly we want to thank the Satterwhites, Kimmerers, Holly Allen and Maralyn Crosetto for pulling all of us together to honour and celebrate Hester. What a beautiful event with every detail perfect, just like Hester loved it. Hester was my sister and my best friend, and I know many of you feel like she was your sister and your best friend too, and I find that very comforting. Hester and I spoke or emailed every day and there was nothing that we couldn't share. I agree with everything that you've all said about her and I so miss her energy, humour, passion, concern for others, and brilliance, every single day. There is a huge hole in my life, and my heart. But I want to thank all of you. We all know that when you had a relationship with Hester she gave 150 percent. She was larger than life, and she gave everything to each and every one of us. But over the years, I have heard so much about all of you, and know that you all gave Hes so much love and support. And in my darkest moments, other than my family and close friends and extended family who have helped to buoy me up, the other saving grace is knowing what all of you meant to her. I can never thank you enough for that. Thank you.

Tricia Rooney Budd and Family

My family and I had the pleasure of meeting Hester a couple of years ago when she did a book signing in the area. She also joined us for dinner at our home and met with my mother and one of my brothers, as well as, my book club. She was a good friend to Tim and it meant a great deal to us that she spent time with us.

Marilla Satterwhite

Skip and I only got to know Hester well in the last ten or eleven years after she came to live in our small mother-in-law apartment at Ballard. I recognize we are very new friends – as many of you may be. But I also know from looking recently at a list of guests who were at Hester's wedding that many of you were old and treasured friends 27 years ago and some of you, of course go back much, much further. I was surprised by this new friendship. Somehow, she worked her way deep into my heart and there we were.

What can I say to give comfort to myself? The last eleven years of Hester's life were turbulent. But I was lucky to have had that time with her. We saw each other a lot. We would talk on the phone for ages - as she did with so many of you - and then we would say, "Do you want to come up? Do you want to come down? Cup of tea? Glass of wine?" (And the wine she had was always wonderful – recommendations from Norman usually)

Many Saturday mornings we would try to pace energetically out to Golden Gardens or up to Café Fiore. There were dozens and dozens of trips to the airport with HUGE unbelievably heavy suitcases, Hester desperately persuading herself and me that she had really pared down this time…. Always traveling to see you all. Combining all book trips with keeping in touch with you – in California, North Carolina, Rhode Island, Minnesota. Meetings at SeaTac and downtown hotels to meet those of you who were here on business – Trisha, Sylvia…

She was a perfectionist as we all know. Nothing was superficial in Hester's life. Nothing was too good, too right for a friend, or for a cousin, niece, brother-in-law, sister, whether it was <u>the</u> card (where <u>did</u> she find them?), searching for the birthday cake from White City which gushed milk, the perfect marzipan torte from miles away on the Eastside.

Any moment was right for dropping everything to care for someone, whether it was in Vancouver, Winnipeg, Toronto, South Lake Union or New Zealand.

While looking at her wedding notebook I saw some words that she had prepared for her address at her wedding. Sadly, that one relationship ended so painfully but we all know that her friendships did not end. At that time, she thanked her friends and family for being such a source of love and warmth to her.

"I shall continue," she said, "to return that love and warmth to all of you, my dearest friends, old and new, my most treasured family, old and new." And that is just what she did.

Skip Satterwhite

I'm Skip and my wife is Marilla. We have a small apartment in our house that Hester lived in for about 10 years. This arrangement was much more than a tenant and landlord relationship. Sound carries through the floor, and we were at least aware of the frequency of conversations and their earnestness. I can assure you that Hester's interchanges were 99% happy talk - animated and sincere as she connected and reached out for hours in the day to friends and family.

She gave new meaning to the word ,"digression". For Hester no story was simply on point, something that most people struggle to make interesting - her memories and her web of personalities was so vast and her awareness for people's relationships was so intertwined that these flooded in as the narrative progressed.

Oh, wait, which reminds me of a story.......No, I can't tell it like she could.

THE PERFECT GIFT

Zanna Satterwhite

If I had one word to describe Hester, it would be "wise." Maybe partly because she had to endure health problems and a divorce. But also because she lived a life full of rich, varied experiences. We asked Hester to marry us and she took the responsibility very seriously. Radiologist, sailor, author, minister.

Hester may have thought of herself as a third wheel in our Seattle family – the Kimmerers and the Satterwhites. At our family gatherings she would sometimes feel bad for herself. I only realized after her death that she was the glue that held us together, the sparky family member who added so much to the gathering-together tradition.

She knew all of our strengths and our weaknesses so well, and didn't have the baggage of being blood-related. She was always there to lend an unbiased ear, and then give sound advice. Hester wanted to be a mother but was never able to – this added to her strength, wisdom, and perspective. She could be the younger generation's confidante – somehow she seemed ageless and able to blend in with any age group. A magical combination of experienced, wise, spontaneous, and fun-loving. Since Hester has left us, family gatherings are not at all the same - a little lacklustre and empty.

I miss Hester's spark of humor and love for the absurd and whimsical. She was the kind of person who would be making people laugh with witty jokes and staying "with it" until she is 100+. Up to date with the latest trends and politics just by being Hester.

She was interesting and never boring. A talented storyteller with stories that would go on and on. Always had interesting things to interject into conversations. Loved to listen to the radio and loved independent films. Loved music and dancing and was up for anything! Staying out at night, taking a zumba class, being open-minded, flying to Veracruz to learn Spanish. She introduced me to jezebel.com, a junky celebrityish but feminist-leaning website, something she knew I could appreciate.

She sincerely cared about people and was interested in people. Choosing out carefully crafted presents, preparing carefully crafted hors d'oeuvres. She had a very generous heart. I complimented her once on her smell of her hair. She then produced a "Cashmere Mist" conditioner sample for me. Today I can wear it and remember her.

Sometimes I would help her with little tasks – finding recordings or articles, washing her car, helping her figure out a computer bug. At the back of my mind I would think, does she really need help with this, or is she just letting me help her so that I will feel better about myself? Hester, I miss you so much.

John Sleavin (CH)

I am John Sleavin, Judy's brother-in law. Hester became a big part of Judy's life, long before the tragedy. Hester was a really big part of the village it took to rebuild Judy, and there is a part of Hester that still lives in that because of how Judy is doing. She really helped bring Judy back in a tough time. Clearly she was someone who Judy trusted with her story. Judy had a lot of big name authors that came to her because it was a story that had pizzazz, that they could sell. She had to have someone she could trust, and of course it was Hester. I got to know Hester through all that, and I heard stories about it through the years.

I think in all of us Hester is still living on, all these stories, and definitely in Judy and how she helped her go on. The storytelling that Hester could do was great- it went on and on. I think there was only one time I didn't appreciate it too much, this is when it was still 'legal' to talk on a cell phone while driving, but still not advisable. She was researching some facts on the book and wanted to talk to me more about some of the things that had gone on and I said "while I'm driving lets keep it short" I kept saying that for 45 minute. Finally I got her off the phone I said, "you know, I gotta pull over. There is a cop behind me, with it's lights on." I was not paying attention to my driving, so she drove me right off the road. I think that was probably the only time I didn't appreciate her ability to spin a story too much. A lot of thanks for everything that Hester has done- it helped a lot of us. Thank you.

Judy Sleavin

My apologies for not being with you all today, I am with my elderly mother as she moves into assisted living in Walnut Creek, CA.

I miss Hester. A few days ago was Annie Rose's Birthday, a day that we always spent together, whether it be in California, or Portland, or on the phone, Hester was always there. I knew I wanted Hester to be my child's god mother, what a great role model she was, intelligent, strong, beautiful, funny, a strong Jewish identity: to me, Hester could do 'anything she set her mind to'. I remember when Annie Rose was born, Hester was sailing in the South Pacific, there was a ham radio connection soon after the birth and I was able to share the joy of Annie Rose with her. What a joyful day, to hear her voice and to know that little Annie Rose would be surrounded with Hester's love, for years to come. Annie Rose was surrounded by Hester's love, and I believe she still is.

We met many years ago, I think it was 1978 when I met John who had come down to our boat to photograph it, he said 'you would love my girlfriend, Hester', and he was right. Hester and I became immediate friends. I never laughed so hard in my life.

Halloween Party in San Francisco, Castro District, with 250,000 costumed to the max, Hester and I dressed as fortune tellers, turbans, and a crystal ball, Hester telling drag queens, as she caressed the crystal ball 'I just KNEW you were going to wear that dress tonight! They loved her, as we all did.

We spent four days in Rotorua, New Zealand, at a Salsa and Samba Festival, going to every dance workshop that was offered, Brazilian Samba, Cuban Salsa.... We danced and laughed and danced and laughed and tried to keep up with the rest of the people, who were half our age. We each lost about 10 pounds that weekend, wore the bottom of our feet off and laughed till we cried. The Wild Girls of New Zealand soon fell in love with Hester and she became a member, bringing a new dimension to our crazy meetings.

I asked Hester to write my story; I trusted her completely and knew that she could do it. I couldn't, it was too hard. Hester said she wasn't a writer, but I knew she was a fantastic story teller. Hester and I would spend hours talking about every little detail of the ordeal and then when it got too difficult for me; we would cry and then end up laughing. She always had that ability. The journey that we took together, for that book, was beautiful, deep, enlightening… she brought insight into my feelings and helped me understand what I was going through. Through her writing she pulled it all together and it is a testament to her that she completed it and had several top publishers in a bidding war over it, an incredible accomplishment. To me, Ten Degrees of Reckoning is about friendship and love.

And that about sums it up, Hester was about friendship and love. With love forever to my dear friend, Hester.

Judy Sleavin

Hester changed my life in ways that are still being revealed. So many things in my life have been affected by something she said, something she sang, the way she danced, cried laughed.

For the year since her untimely passing, she has been 'with me' daily, reliving moments in our lives, with a full range of feelings from sharing deep despair to absolutely laughing till we couldn't stop. I saw her in so many things, so many places, it was like she wasn't gone from my life, but still here with me.

We salsa'd for three days straight , in N.Z. She bought me a Mark Anthony CD; I can't salsa or listen to salsa music without smiling, thinking about those three days. Hester redefined friendship, helped me understand my feelings, pulled me up when I fell down. I don't know the words to describe the beauty of the friendship. She will always be with me. She will always be with Annie Rose.

THE PERFECT GIFT

Peter van der Ven & Margreet de Leeuw

This is where Bear came from. When Hester was about to sail to New Zealand in 1987, she met Margreet's stuffed bear, named Bear. Bear had a space at the back of his head that allowed you to put your hand inside and move his face and mouth. He was (and still is) charming and expressive, and Hester took a great liking to him. We thought an adventurous bear might make a good sailing companion. Knowing that space aboard Shahar was at a premium, we acquired Bear's younger, smaller brother who, oddly, also turned out to be named Bear. I know, it's a bit confusing. Being smaller, he didn't have the same hand space inside for creating facial movements, but he turned out to have a great talent of his own for creative expression and communication.

When we presented the junior Bear to Hester, she was informed that there wasn't room for such an extravagance aboard a 26 foot sailboat. Curses! Margreet and I considered...we didn't want to have the little guy looking at us sadly the whole time Hester was gone. That would be a long time. There had to be another way. We made him a passport and decided to sneak him aboard Shahar as a stowaway. Somehow, I finagled the combination to the cabin door lock, and under cover of darkness the night before the voyage began, we carefully hid Bear on Shahar.

I guess once Bear was there, the captain didn't have the heart to throw him overboard. Bear kept quiet in the beginning, but we were told that one magical day, Bear spoke up during a dispute. He went on to develop his gift for expressing someone's difficult feelings in a non-threatening way. This earned him a place as ship's counsel and general dear friend. Somewhere along the way, he found another, smaller brother, Bud, and I think Hester found a third bear to round out her band, who proudly occupied a place of honor at the head of her bed.

I hope they've found an excellent home. I'm sure if you listen carefully, Bear can tell you tale after tale – he probably has Hester's amazing gift for telling a story, and he's seen a lot more than many of us will in his voyages over the seas and various ports, villages, families, and children, through Hester's eyes. Please take good care of him, and make sure he has plenty of tee shirts.

Peter van der Ven

I met Hester shortly after coming to the Oral Medicine Department at the University of Washington in 1987. We met reviewing pathology slides with one of my classmates, Andrea. Hester invited me to see a Dutch movie. She told me her Mum was a first cousin of Moe Howard (of the Three Stooges). When I was growing up, the Three Stooges were something that my dad and I were able to bond over, and I have a huge soft spot for them. Actually meeting one of their relatives felt a little magical to me, a bit of fairy dust. She told me about her near-death experience on the operating table. She drove an old, orange VW Rabbit on whose hood Rob Kimmerer had rubbed a heart that never washed away. She always brought you a gift, something that mattered, even if it was small.

I feel called to say that Hester was one of the kindest, most generous people I have ever met. Maybe it was from her lifelong suffering with Crohn's, but she had a level of genuine empathy and a sense of fairness that she extended to practically everyone, matched only by her sense of humor and ability to hold an audience of one or a hundred in the palm of her hand when she told a story. I wish she were here to see the beginnings of the Occupy movement. I think she'd have been very excited about it. My take home message, my way to remember her, is to try every day to do at least one thing for someone else that I might not otherwise have done, but Hester might have – and to not put things off, because life is too precious and short. I miss you my friend.

Joel Wardinger

From all that has been said today about Auntie Hester, the overarching theme that we can tease out is that she was a paragon of "Chesed" - loving kindness. Extending herself beyond normal boundaries for other people. Every single person who is now mourning her loss surely can recount a number of personal stories where they were touched by her Chesed. That is her legacy and it is that overwhelming concern for others that we have lost today.

Our great Sages of the Talmud relate that among the precepts whose fruits a person enjoys in This World, but whose principal remains intact for him or her in the World to Come, we find: Honoring one's parents, acts of kindness, hospitality, visiting the sick, and helping to bury the deceased.

Examples abound:

Honoring Parents: Auntie Hester was in Toronto specifically for the purpose of taking care of her mother, Bubs. Distance would not prevent her from being there for her parents when they needed support.

Acts of Kindness: Whoever received a gift from Auntie Hester that was not unique, not perfect, not totally in tune with the recipient's totality of being- Impossible. She must have spent so much time merely conjuring up the perfect thing for her intended recipient. Her desire to benefit others and to bring happiness to the world was almost odd in its creativity and depth.

Hospitality to guests: Boy, was it beyond the norm - when me and my crew of scraggly friends showed up to shack up with Auntie Hester in our gap year before university. How she overextended herself for us and how she tended to our every interest has left a lasting impression on me, and my friends who got to witness real hospitality.

Bikur Cholim/Tending to the Sick: Putting aside her own health issues, Auntie Hester made super-human efforts in tending to the needs of others close to her. When Uncle Ross grew increasingly weakened by illness, Auntie Hester grabbed the reins, and invested time and love in ensuring things went easily and smoothly. She did the same for her niece, my cousin, Naomi in her long battle with cancer.

Burying the Deceased: When it came to the most difficult and wrenching tasks, of course Auntie Hester was there as well. The tragic death of my Uncle Ross, her brother, propelled her into action, to make all of the arrangements and to ensure that everything be done respectfully, properly, and solemnly. This is one of the greatest Mitzvot that exists, and is described by our Rabbis as, *Chessed Shel Emes*, the purest form of loving-kindness, because it is something that cannot be repaid.

This week's Torah portion relates how immediately after discussing the use of Para Adumah [Red Heifer] ashes to purify a person who came into contact with the dead, the Torah tells us of the death of Miriam [Bamidbar 20:1]. The Talmud says that the juxtaposition of these two portions teaches that "Just as the Para Adumah atones, so too the death of a righteous person atones".

The death of a righteous person, somehow, atones because the spiritual legacy of a righteous person leaves an indelible mark upon all those they touched. Their ascent to Heaven, and their leaving this world, beckons us to live up to the defining message of their life.

Auntie Hester defined Chessed. We must learn from her life and integrate her message in the fabric of our own. As we now embark on this gruelling task of burying Auntie Hester, may we strive to strengthen our own resolve to bring love and kindness to the world, the way she did, and in so doing, raise her soul ever higher.

THE PERFECT GIFT

Marisa Wardinger

I'm still in disbelief that I have to think of Auntie Hester in past tense right now. Life, for Joel, Alison and I has always included Hester. And not just as another aunt who visited from time to time, but as our mother's sister and best friend who treated us, supported us, and loved us like we were her own children. She always made sure to take an interest in everything that was going on in our lives, what we were studying, where we were traveling. And for Hes, that interest was not obligatory- it was true, genuine and authentic in every way. And she was like this with everyone she met. I can recall so many times when upon introducing her to friends of mine, I'd watch in awe at how engaging she was, how truly interested she was in getting to know the people who were close to me. Partly because of her genuine interest in others, and partly -I think - because if she got to know the people in MY life, her connection to ME would be that much stronger. And she always made me feel like that was a priority for her.

But Hester wasn't just a PART of my life in a major way, I am certain that she changed my life in major ways. I grew up seeing her between trips to exotic places, hearing stories of her adventures on the high seas and on remote islands. How amazing I would think to myself. How inspiring. It was only a matter of time before I would catch that wanderlust bug. But traveling on my own was not easy at first. In fact there were many moments that I wanted to give up, and head home. And then midway through my first big trip, Hes met me in New Zealand, where I spent a week living on her 26 foot boat. I remember thinking after 2 or 3 days on that boat- my aunt is a crazy person! How does she live like this? And the answer is simple- Hester could take on any challenge, turn any tough situation into a positive and even exhilarating experience- that was Hester. I am sure I would be the crazy one had I not followed in her footsteps and taken advantage of seeing the world like she did.

And then there was that time in my life about 7 years ago - after all the traveling- when I had no definite plans for a future career. And I remember telling Hes, during one of our lengthy phone conversations, that what I'd really love to do is take a month long training to become a Yoga instructor. Problem was, I had just spent all my money traveling, and wasn't sure I could afford to do it. Without any hesitation, Hester said- you have to do it, and I'm going to help you. And again, that was Hester. It was like, OK, Marisa... you have a dream... you go for it.... and I will do what's necessary to make that happen for you. And 7 years later, I own a Yoga studio- an achievement that would not have been possible without her support, her trust, and wholehearted belief in me.

In contemplating this incredible loss we are experiencing right now, I find myself searching for answers and then reflecting on life in general. And the idea of impermanence comes to mind. The idea that change is about the only guarantee life offers us. And then I think about Hester's life, and how compared to most, Hester's life was filled with impermanence. And despite the impermanence of her life, there are so many people in this room today that no matter what, could count on Hester. We could count on her to be there no matter what tough times she might be going through, to be generous no matter how little she had, and to help make our own tough times a little brighter. Without Hester, there is a very real hole in many of our lives- something clearly missing. But while she's not here in the way we wish she was at this moment, I do believe that along with the inspiring legacy she leaves behind, she is ever present in our hearts and minds, and that is a comfort. And despite the impermanence of life in general, we can count on that. We can count on the memories, the laughter we shared, the love and support that was always apparent. And if I can pass all of that on to my kids, with Auntie Hester's spirit in mind, she will really never leave us.

Wild Girls (Val Boag, Jigs Bradley, Judy (Jemma) Dempster, Heather Gollop, Babe Moratti, Judy Sleavin, Leanne Wallace)

Hester… friend, confidante, fun-loving, vivacious, courageous, articulate, author, researcher, loyal, generous…these were just some of the words the Wild Girls offered to describe this beautiful woman. We were gathered at Jemma's seaside 'bach'…the 'Cheetah Retreat' for our annual Christmas get-together. Val, Jigs, Heather, Jemma, Leanne and Babe. Missing was Judy, now residing in America. Seven girls whose lives have been touched and enhanced by Hester.

As we recalled our first meeting with Hester and the impression she made on us all, we remembered the excitement we felt each time we heard that she was returning to N.Z. Little did we know that the last time would be the last one. The hugs, the kisses, the feeling of genuine friendship remain with us, as will her stories, her impersonations, her ability to make us laugh and her generosity of gifts for each of us. Thanks to Hester the Wild Girls became Cheetah Girls or Cheetah Wild Girls. We delight in wearing cheetah print clothes and jewellery and carrying cheetah handbags and cosmetic bags...every item a reminder of Hester's kindness.

Jemma has planted a N.Z. native kauri tree on her farm in Hester's memory. The kauri tree will stand as a living memorial to Hester. Jemma invites all who read this book to come, stay and wander over the farm to where our Wild Girl tribute to Hester is planted. The plaque reads...

"Our Canadian Wild Girl... Darling Hester. Dr. Hester Rumberg 7~08~1947 - 26~06~2011.

Our tribute was not as great as Hester's tribute to her dear friend Judy. As a family friend and Godmother to Annie, the sailing tragedy affected Hester greatly. She undertook the hard work to promote safety at sea through the Sleavin Family Foundation. Then later, writing on behalf of Judy, the book "Ten Degrees of Reckoning".

Together with Judy and Hester we learnt more about Jewish celebrations... Yom Kippur, Bat Mitzvah, Hanukka...taking part in candle lighting, scrumptious feasts and dancing holding hands in a circle to Hava Nagila! Watching "Fiddler on the Roof" for the 'umpteenth' time and singing "If I were a Rich Man"! And we yelled "Mazel Tov" on our evenings of fun at Judy's apartment ~ enhanced by a wine or two!

Our admiration for Hester grew when she co-ordinated the events to mark the ten year anniversary of Judy's loss. Hester organised the venue, chose the music and oversaw the entire occasion. Nothing was left out, and happiness mixed with sadness ensued when friends gathered to lend Judy support.

When researching for the book, which she wrote on behalf of Judy, Hester was meticulous in her steps to track down the key people involved in Judy's rescue.

In Russell, in the Bay of Islands she learnt that one of the men who responded to the alert when Judy was spotted from a Search and Rescue plane, was working on a construction site. Nothing for Hester to climb scaffolding, clamber over building supplies to reach her reluctant hero! A few reassuring words from Hester and trust was gained and as it was close to "knock off" time he offered her a beer and the two sat on beer crates, drinking beer from the bottle while Hester asked questions and listened to his story.

When the Maori community closest to Deep Water Cove where Judy was washed ashore, wanted to embrace Judy and her family and accept them into their hapu (sub-tribe), Hester was invited to speak on the Rawhiti marae (meeting place) as spokesperson for Judy. This was an honour and privilege as it is not usual protocol for women to speak on a marae. Both Hester and Judy appreciated the warmth and humanity shown by our Maori people.

Music was important to Hester and with Jemma on recorder or tin whistle, Hester on ukulele, and the rest of us on an assortment of percussion instruments, we had fun "jamming" with her whether in someone's home or busking on the roadside!

THE PERFECT GIFT

Hester once told us she was related to the Three Stooges; if this is true it explains her ability to tell funny stories and articulate so well the typical New York accent of these comedians. She had us in fits of laughter with her impersonations! Ian and Babe had three sheep on their property and Hester aptly named them Larry, Curly and Moe after the Three Stooges!

Naturally we have all read Hester's book, "Ten Degrees of Reckoning" and acknowledge her skill in her research and ability to choose words so sensitively in describing some of the horrific events. Despite being emotionally involved with the Sleavin family, her ability to write such a moving story the way she has, is admired by us all.

Hester has left us her 'perfect gift'…a memory of a life lived to the full, of fun and laughter, intelligent conversation, sincere empathy for others yet coping with her own health problem so bravely, and last but not least …of deep friendship.

We close with one of Hester's favourite quotes…."We are connected in mystery and miracle to each other and to the universe". Rest in Peace Hester.

Hester's speech at the Sleavin memorial

On Judith's behalf, welcome and thank you so much for your presence here today. Ten years ago, not far from the site of this beautiful & serene home, a tragedy occurred, a tragedy of such momentous proportions to make the marking of time meaningless. All the same, an anniversary of ten years' time must not go unnoticed or unobserved. More importantly for Judith, there has never been a formal occasion to mourn the deaths of her family. Judy was hospitalized at the time of the memorial services in Opua and in the United States, and later, in place of the rituals of the scattering of ashes or the unveiling of headstones, there was a coroner's inquest. And so we are gathered here today, to mourn, to commemorate, to celebrate this glorious family.

The one remarkable and positive result of this heart-breaking event was Judy coming to your shores and into your lives, and you into hers. A new community was created, one in which I am so proud and honoured to participate in, and to share today with each of you.

As we remember this terrible loss, it is possible to feel that nothing we can do or say is up to the task. Indeed, even today's gathering is a bit tentative in nature, but as always, we will trust that our communal love and support can counter any bumps in the road, and that together we can find a way to heal Judy and each other.

The only traditional part will be the following, called the Kaddish, which is transliterated to allow you to follow along. This prayer is said at the time of death and at every anniversary thereafter. It is meant to turn each mourner's thoughts to a serious affirmation to make a better life on earth and to honour those who are still here. It teaches us to enrich ourselves through treating each other kindly and through faith and through the spiritual aspects of our lives.

KADDISH

Grieving is universal. Let us take two minutes to think of all the dearly departed in our lives.

SHALOM ALEICHEM

Some leaves are allowed to age and turn colours and fall naturally to the ground. Others are ripped too early from the trees. Nevertheless, while they remain they nourish us with their beauty and oxygen and radiance.

All of us, this community of friends, this family that you have created, promise to keep you in our hearts forever. We promise to move on with you, we promise to step back with you when you need us. We promise we will never forget your family in the universe around us, nor will we ever forget to tell you how immeasurably grateful we are to have you here with us on earth, in this wonderful world.

20 Things About Me – PeggyLeeWannaBe
Wordsmoker.com August 19, 2009

1. I'll never be able to contribute enough to get into the top twenty list of Wordsmoker commenters. I'm more of a voyeur.

2. I had a very decent professional life until I got bored, bored, bored, and then I literally sailed off into the sunset. This was the extreme of any camping trip or intense sporting life. Since I consider myself happiest when I'm walking through Manhattan or Sydney or any interesting urban environment, I really don't know how it was I undertook so much effort to make this happen. Or why I took such tremendous delight in its success.

3. My now ex-husband deserted the sinking ship after 40,000 miles at sea when a woman asked him to join her band (not the Seven Dwarfs or the Lost Boys, but a real band.)

4. I wrote a book that was published this year, but I'm enchanted by the lot that share on this site. Some of your comments are easily more pithy, profound, laugh-out-loud, and erudite than many a paragraph in my book.

5. You're also kind (don't deny it); I am too.

6. My maternal grandmother was the second youngest of many siblings who arrived at Ellis Island from Lithuania. Her eldest brother started the trend years before she came. He was the father of Moe, Shemp and Curly Howard. Since there was a very large age gap between my mother and her first cousins, I was myself way too young, too Canadian, and too female to know or appreciate anything about them. But I do have family pictures. Hopefully no resemblance, since we stay away from

full bangs and crew cuts. Just reporting some genealogy, although I have never brought this fact up in any conversation that I can recall.

6. I have now lived as long in the USA as in my birthplace, Canada, and I have sailed to countless countries. It is disconcerting to find myself with no strong patriotic attitude. This doesn't mean that I am without undeniable political leanings, nor does it mean that I am incapable of feeling alternatively proud or ashamed or bemused at specific occurrences. But it does mean that I often experience a sense of looking from the outside in wherever I am.

7. I have dealt with chronic problems from an immune disease present since birth, not visible to the naked eye, so I "suffer" in silence. I was hospitalized many times in my younger years, and I have had one very real out of body experience.

8. Despite the above, I am not a religious person at all. I don't mind when other people take comfort in religion, as long as they're not extremists, don't foist their beliefs on me, and aren't waiting until they get to heaven to live as they should right here in the present tense.

9. I intensely dislike the word impact since its evolution into a verb.

10. I have cobbled together an extraordinary little family of friends of all ages in the city in which I live. I love them fiercely and I am loved by them. Still, I imagine that I fall into the category of people who sometimes have nowhere to go, as Mama Penguino described.

11. My sister and I always shared a bedroom, consigned to this horrible fate by our parents. Just because we were one year apart I suppose they thought we would enjoy each other's company. We didn't, and the proximity of our heads each night, and the lack of privacy only added to our mutual perception that we lived on very different planets of reality. Now we do reside in different countries, and different coasts. Nonetheless, we are each other's best friend, and we speak on the phone every single day, starting most conversations with, so anyway…..

12. I am a fairly good judge of character, and I live regularly by my instincts. Even my ex-husband had many redeeming qualities, and mostly I chose him for his Peter Pan-like existence. I wanted adventure at the time.

13. I am not a very practical person, and all my downfalls are because of this deficiency.

14. I need to learn to speak Spanish before I die. I won't be a complete person or discover my entire personality without this language. I do not know where this aspiration comes from, and I don't care to dissect it, I just know it is a deep desire within my soul.

15. A few months ago I was standing in a deli in Chicago ready to order a takeaway meal. The man behind the counter asked what I wanted and I told him that the guy beside me was there first. The guy turned to me and said, "thanks, but I've already ordered." I'm sorry to say that I practically shrieked and asked, are you Jermaine? As in Jemaine (no R) in Flight of the Conchords. It was indeed him, but where was

my cool? ? (editor's note: A New Zealand-based comedy duo composed of Bret McKenzie and Jemaine Clement.)

16. I have fair skin and freckles, and I am not as easily amused in summer as I am in the other seasons of the year.

17. When I first began to watch The Wire, I thought I might need subtitles. Then I got into the rhythm of it, and stayed in for five days watching the first three seasons on DVD. I've now finished watching all five seasons, as well as every episode of Homicide: Life on the Street. I think this rules out a diagnosis of ADHD, but what about addictive personality disorder? I'm afraid to begin Mad Men.

18. I'm a very poor sleeper and I always have been. I know I need more sleep to prolong my life, but who needs a long life of tossing and turning.

19. I have shed most of my Canadiana reserve, but I have never (yet) winked at anyone.

20. My mother continues to repeat to her grown children, "If stands in the corner stiff" whenever we go off half-cocked. I have heard this reflective statement from my mother since I could tie my own shoelaces, and unhappily, I still don't live wholly by it.

Dr. Hester Rumberg to Receive 2009 Award (University of Manitoba, Sept 14, 2009)

Dr. Hester Rumberg has been named the winner of the 2009 Alumni of Distinction award. The honor is awarded each year by the Faculty of Dentistry and School of Dental Hygiene. "The selection committees were impressed by the body of work of this individual in terms of her contribution to the profession and to the community as a whole, which is the main criteria of this award," said Scott Leckie, president of the University of Manitoba Dental Alumni Association and a member of the dentistry selection committee.

Hester Rumberg is an alumnus of the University of Manitoba's School of Dental Hygiene, Class of 1969. Rumberg began her Dental Hygiene career working in periodontics and later on taught at the University of British Columbia's Faculty of Dentistry. She went on to earn a dental degree at the University of Washington specializing in oral and maxillofacial radiology, and has become a sought-after speaker on oral health issues, particularly for dental hygiene groups. Most recently, Rumberg published her first novel – the true story of a tragic loss at sea – that led to her creation of the Sleavin Family Foundation, a non-profit organization dedicated to promoting maritime safety throughout the world.

The Seattle Times July 21, 2011

Hester Rumberg died unexpectedly in her sleep on Sunday, June 26, 2011 while visiting family in Toronto. Her loving heart and joyful spirit touched people wherever she traveled. Always thoughtful of others, Hester served up her boundless love with graciousness, generosity and style. Born August 7, 1947 in Winnipeg Manitoba, graduate of the Universities of Manitoba and Washington and a Board-Certified Oral/Maxillofacial Radiologist, Dr. Rumberg taught on the faculty of Oral Medicine at the University of Washington School Of Dentistry from 1983 to 1998 receiving noteworthy adoration from her students. An experienced offshore sailor, Capt. Rumberg skippered her small sailboats to Hawaii, remote islands, New Zealand and Australia. Treasured friend of the Sleavin family, Hester changed the direction of her life when their family suffered a tragedy at sea. She and Judith Sleavin established the Sleavin Family Foundation, promoting maritime safety. Hester's widely praised book, "Ten Degrees of Reckoning", the story of that disaster at sea, stands as a remarkable tribute to the resilience of not only the Sleavins but to her own courageous choices in life. Daughter of Betty and the late Joseph Rumberg. Sister and sister-in-law of Susan and Alan Roadburg, and the late, Ross Rumberg. A Memorial Service and burial were held in Toronto at Beth Tikvah Synagogue and Pardes Shalom Cemetery on Wednesday, June 29th. Her friends are invited to celebrate Hester's life at an event in Seattle on October 15.

The Many Sides of Hester

You Tube interview
https://www.youtube.com/watch?v=DsyU7kbC8dg

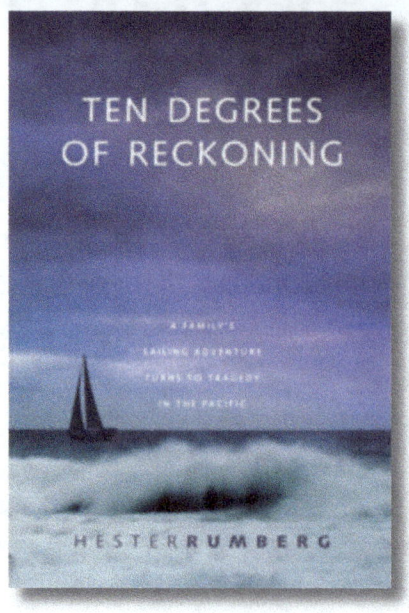

THE PERFECT GIFT

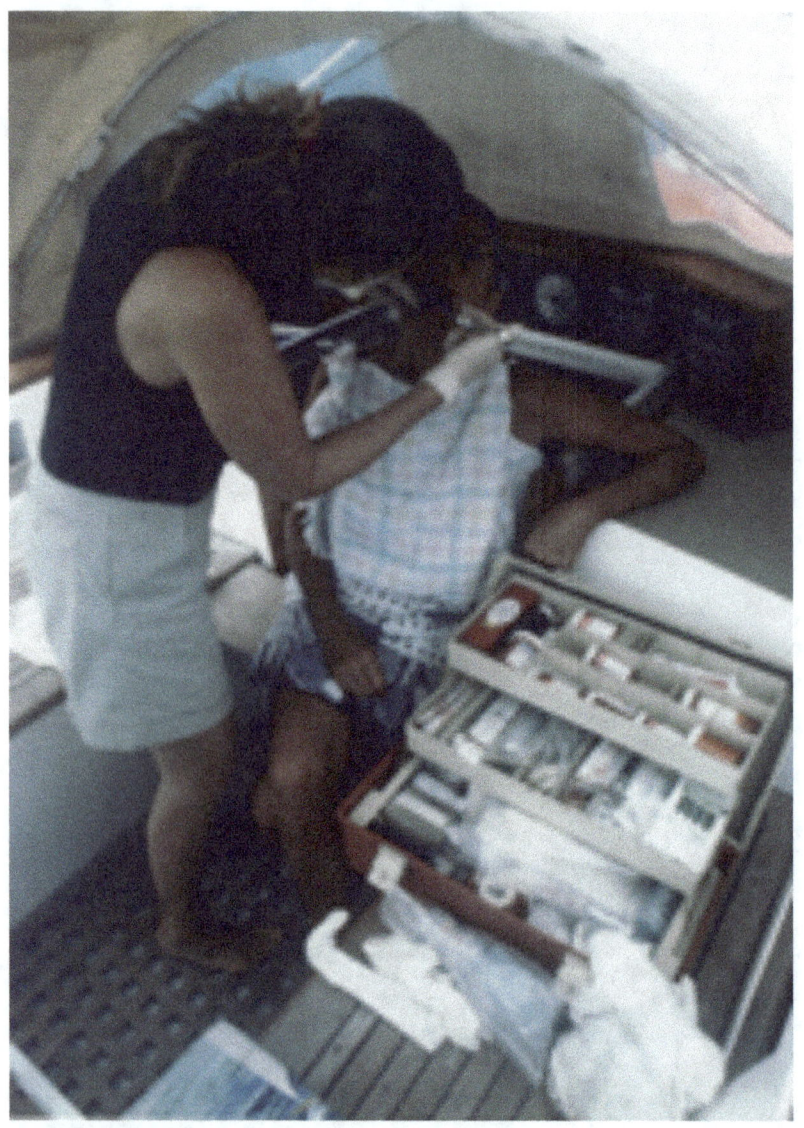

THE PERFECT GIFT

www.ingramcontent.com/pod-product-compliance
Lightning Source LLC
Chambersburg PA
CBHW052028290426
44112CB00014B/2418